CAREERS MAKING A DIFFERENCE

HELPING VICTIMS

CAREERS MAKING A DIFFERENCE

HELPING ANIMALS

HELPING CHILDREN

HELPING SENIORS

HELPING THOSE IN POVERTY

HELPING THOSE WITH ADDICTIONS

HELPING THOSE WITH DISABILITIES

HELPING THOSE WITH MENTAL ILLNESSES

HELPING TO PROTECT THE ENVIRONMENT

HELPING VICTIMS

CAREERS MAKING A DIFFERENCE

HELPING VICTIMS

AMANDA TURNER

MASON CREST

PHILADELPHIA
MIAMI

MASON CREST

450 Parkway Drive, Suite D, Broomall, Pennsylvania 19008
(866) MCP-BOOK (toll-free) • www.masoncrest.com

Printed in the United States of America

First printing
9 8 7 6 5 4 3 2 1

ISBN (hardback) 978-1-4222-4262-9
ISBN (series) 978-1-4222-4253-7
ISBN (ebook) 978-1-4222-7548-1

Cataloging-in-Publication Data on file with the Library of Congress

Developed and produced by National Highlights Inc.
Editor: Susan Uttendorfsky
Interior and cover design: Torque Advertising + Design
Production: Michelle Luke

TABLE OF CONTENTS

KEY ICONS TO LOOK FOR

Words to Understand: These words with their easy-to-understand definitions will increase the reader's understanding of the text while building vocabulary skills.

Sidebars: This boxed material within the main text allows readers to build knowledge, gain insights, explore possibilities, and broaden their perspectives by weaving together additional information to provide realistic and holistic perspectives.

Educational Videos: Readers can view videos by scanning our QR codes, providing them with additional educational content to supplement the text. Examples include news coverage, moments in history, speeches, iconic sports moments, and much more!

Text-Dependent Questions: These questions send the reader back to the text for more careful attention to the evidence presented there.

Research Projects: Readers are pointed toward areas of further inquiry connected to each chapter. Suggestions are provided for projects that encourage deeper research and analysis.

Series Glossary of Key Terms: This back-of-the-book glossary contains terminology used throughout this series. Words found here increase the reader's ability to read and comprehend higher-level books and articles in this field.

AWARENESS OF THE CAUSE

Crime is a major public health issue affecting mental, physical, emotional, financial, and spiritual health. It is only relatively recently that victims are now being supported as they should be. Fortunately, though, increased energies into public and personal safety has also facilitated crime prevention, too. Following a crime, it is now widely understood how important it is for the victim to be helped and guided through a period of peace and healing.

"No one is useless in this world who lightens the burdens of another."
– Charles Dickens

"Our laws must protect victims."
– Theresa May
(British prime minister)

"For too long, the victims of crime have been the forgotten persons of our criminal justice system."
– Ronald Reagan

"Always the innocent are the first victims, so it has been for ages past, so it is now."
– J.K. Rowling

CHAPTER 1

Is a Career in Victim Advocacy For You?

Most people have a worthy cause that they believe in. You can even work in this field yourself by following a career and making a difference to those in need.

- Start out as a volunteer.
- Seek out personal connection in the field.
- Develop an inspirational mission statement for yourself.
- Find out about the education, training and qualifications required for your chosen career.
- Study job specifications of interest.
- Discuss your goals with your loved ones.
- Approach school counselors, charities, and organizations to obtain advice.

AWARENESS OF THE CAUSE

FBI STATISTICS

According to recent FBI annual statistics, both violent crime and property crime have declined in the last year.

PROPERTY CRIME

The recent FBI report also showed there were more than 7.7 million property crimes last year. Burglaries decreased 7.6 percent, and larceny-thefts decreased 2.2 percent. Motor vehicle thefts increased 0.8 percent.

- Nationwide, there were an estimated 7,694,086 property crimes. The estimated numbers for two of the three property crimes showed declines when compared with the previous year's estimates.

PROPERTY CRIME

Burglary 82.1%

Motor Vehicle Theft 10%

Larceny-Theft 71.2%

- Collectively, victims of property crimes (excluding arson) suffered losses estimated at $15.3 billion.

- The arrest rate for property crime was 388.7 per 100,000 inhabitants.

- Of the property crime offenses, the arrest rate for burglary was 61.7 per 100,000 inhabitants; larceny-theft, 296.0; and motor vehicle theft, 28.2. The arrest rate for arson was 2.8 per 100,000 inhabitants.

Source: FBI crime figures released in 2018.

VIOLENT CRIME

Overall violent crime decreased 0.2 percent from the previous year, while property crime decreased 3 percent during that time, according to Crime in the United States, the FBI's annual compilation of crime statistics.

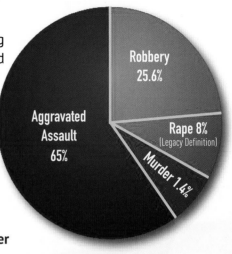

VIOLENT CRIME

- **The most recent statistics reported that there were an estimated 1,247,321 violent crimes. The estimated number of robbery offenses decreased 4.0 percent, and the estimated number of murder and nonnegligent manslaughter offenses decreased 0.7 percent.**

- **Estimated volume of aggravated assault and rape (revised definition) offenses increased 1.0 percent and 2.5 percent, respectively.**

- **The arrest rate for violent crime was 160.7 per 100,000 inhabitants;**

- **The arrest rate for violent crime was 160.7 per 100,000 inhabitants; the arrest rate for property crime was 388.7 per 100,000 inhabitants.**

DID YOU KNOW?

- **Public perceptions about crime in the U.S. often don't align with the data.**

- **There are large geographical variations in crime rates.**

- **Most crimes are not reported to the police, and most reported crimes are not solved.**

- **The FBI estimated law enforcement agencies nationwide made 10.6 million arrests (excluding those for traffic violations).**

AWARENESS OF THE CAUSE

6 Victim Support Services

1 Police

5 Witness Assistance Services

WHERE DOES A VICTIM OF CRIME GO TO GET HELP?

2 Charities

4 Helplines

3 Support Organizations

WHAT TYPES OF HELP SHOULD VICTIMS SEEK?

- Understanding and sympathy
- Information about the crime committed
- Conflict resolution advice
- Emotional help

- Practical help
- Financial help
- Encouragement
- Independent legal advice
- Compensation advice

THE BENEFITS OF HELPING OTHERS

A SENSE OF PURPOSE
Giving to others provides a sense of purpose to an individual. People who volunteer for a cause feel that their life is worthwhile and satisfying. This ultimately leads to improved physical and emotional health.

EMOTIONAL HEALTH
Studies have also shown that the act of charity results in emotional well-being. The person who gives to charity feels improved self-esteem. This gives a feeling of satisfaction to the individual. In a way, giving to others allows the individual to create a "kindness bank account." The more kind acts are filled in the account, the better the emotional state of the person.

A HEALTHY HEART
A recent study found that there is a significant correlation between helping others and the heart's health. It was found that people who volunteer are about 40 percent less likely to develop high blood pressure as compared to those who do not volunteer.

HELPING OTHERS MAKES YOU HAPPY
According to research, people who engage in acts of kindness and giving are happier in general as compared to others. Acts of kindness carried out regularly or even once a week can lead to greater happiness and joy in life.

REDUCE STRESS
The act of helping others can also help reduce stress. Research shows that people who help others have lower cortisol levels. The presence of this hormone in the body creates feelings of anxiety and panic, which can lead to higher blood pressure levels. People who do less for others have a higher level of the stress hormone in their body.

Milestone Moment

ESTABLISHMENT OF THE VINE NETWORK

For many years, victims of crime had to live in constant anxiety, wondering when their assailant would be released from police custody, jail, or prison. In 1994, the VINE network (Victim Information & Notification Everyday) was created to put an end to victims having to live in perpetual fear. This system was established in response to the murder of Mary Byron, who was killed by her former boyfriend shortly after his release from prison. The former boyfriend was in jail for charges of kidnapping and raping Byron, but neither she nor her family was notified when he was released on bail. If they had been notified, perhaps her murder could have been prevented.

Today, most states allow anyone to register for VINE access, which means they will receive an automated phone call when the offender in question is released from custody, with instructions on what to do if they feel that their personal safety is in jeopardy. It's impossible to tell how many lives the VINE system has saved, and its creation was a huge leap for the field of victim advocacy.

VINE (Victim Information & Notification Everyday) allows a victim of a crime to be notified if the perpetrator is released from jail.

WORDS TO UNDERSTAND

advocacy: support for certain individuals, causes, or policies

perpetrator: a person who commits a harmful or illegal act

psychology: the study of the human mind, its functions, and how those functions influence human behavior

trauma: a distressing or disturbing experience, often creating long-lasting psychological effects

CHAPTER 2

What Does a Victim Advocate Do, and Why Do We Need Them?

JOB ROLES AND SPECIFICATIONS

Victim advocates are professionals who are trained to support victims of life-altering crimes. Victim advocates are a link between crime victims and the criminal justice system. Often, when someone is the victim of a crime, life feels overwhelming, and they aren't sure what next steps need to be taken. They might feel powerless and decide that following the path of least resistance—doing nothing—is the easiest way to deal with their **trauma**, leaving the offender on the loose to hurt other people.

A victim advocate is a supportive, listening ear who can guide them in the right direction while giving them valuable advice and access to resources. A professional in this field can work in a variety of settings, such as police offices, courtrooms, counseling centers, crime hotlines, hospitals, and prisons. Many people in this field have specialized training in the areas of **psychology**, counseling, law enforcement, and/or other areas focused on helping people in society. Some are volunteers, and others

WHAT'S BURNOUT?

Burnout is a concern for victim advocates, both those who volunteer and those who are paid. The term refers to a mental collapse due to ongoing job, volunteer, or home life stress. Burnout can make it impossible for a victim advocate to do their job effectively. Sadly, this state is common in fields that ask workers and volunteers to invest emotionally in their work. It is hard to come to work day after day and deal with emotionally taxing situations. Teachers, advocates, law enforcement officers, nurses, and other people who work to help society all have high levels of workplace exhaustion in their fields.

A breakdown can be avoided by taking scheduled days off, not working outside of paid work hours (in other words, not taking work home), seeking counseling for particularly difficult work situations, and speaking with a supervisor if the workload begins to feel too overwhelming.

are paid staff members of organizations created to assist crime victims. All victim advocates have specialized training to allow them to effectively serve crime victims, regardless of their academic training.

A victim advocate can play many roles, including counseling those affected by crime in a one-on-one setting, operating a hotline for victims of violent crime (such as rape, abuse, or hate crimes), going to court with victims to provide emotional support, providing them with resources to help them recover, assisting them with safety planning if they feel threatened, running support groups for those in similar circumstances, and talking with victims about different options that are available in their specific situation and location.

Contrary to popular belief, victim advocates do not tell people what to do or how to feel. They do not coach them to press charges if the victim does not feel comfortable doing so. They simply help people navigate the emotional minefield that tends to come with facing an offender of a life-

Victim advocates are professionals who have been trained to support victims affected by crime. They provide the help and reassurance that a victim needs to recover.

altering crime. Many victims find it difficult to testify against their perpetrator, and an advocate can coach the victim so they feel strong, confident, and powerful enough to overcome their fear and testify in court.

Sometimes victim advocates are able to keep their conversations with clients totally confidential, but this is not always the case. While advocates are committed to keeping victims' privacy a top priority, local and state laws might require that they divulge information to the local police department when necessary. This often depends on the nature of the crime. Domestic violence victim advocates, for example, are exempt from this rule in many states, as reporting the crime could cause the victim further harm. There is some information that advocates must report to authorities, such as threats to a person's safety or neglect/abuse of children.

There are many reasons why people choose to go into the field of victim advocacy. Some have been a victim of a violent crime at some time in their life and they want to use their unique perspective to guide others

There are certain situations when confidentiality is an important aspect of being a victim advocate. Sometimes, it is essential to protect a victim of crime by keeping their personal identity, medical records, immigration status, and other information private.

YOU ARE NOT ALONE

Victim advocates have specialized training in numerous areas so that they can help victims of many different types of crime.

through the process. Some are former law enforcement professionals who see the need for victim support. Some are psychology professionals who want to use their talent and education in a unique way to support those who need it most.

Regardless of how they come to the field, victim advocates

agree that while their job can be difficult and stressful, it's also incredibly important and rewarding. Being a victim advocate can be just as emotionally taxing as it is fulfilling. It's important that these professionals take care of their own mental health, which may involve seeking therapy or talking through particularly difficult work situations with colleagues.

Some victim advocates work with victims of many different types of crime, but most have specialized training in helping with a specific type of crime. Here, we'll discuss the different challenges and responsibilities faced in specific areas of victim advocacy.

ARSON

Usually, arson is defined as a crime in which fire or explosives are used to purposefully damage property or cause personal injury or harm. In many cases of arson, people are hurt or killed and homes and businesses are destroyed. Arson victims deal with a variety of issues, including post-traumatic stress disorder (PTSD). It's often very difficult for victims of arson to stand up to the accused arsonist in court, as this person has typically caused, or attempted to cause, irreparable harm to the victim, their family, and their personal property.

A victim advocate can be an invaluable support for an arson victim. They can walk the person through the Crime Victim Compensation Program in their state. This program

Arson is defined as a crime in which fire or explosives are used to damage property or cause personal injury or harm. This is an extremely serious crime as a victim may lose all their property, be made homeless, injured, or suffer a very painful death.

provides government funding to help reimburse the arson victim for property loss and damage. There is a hefty amount of paperwork involved, and this can feel overwhelming to someone who is already dealing with an extreme loss. An advocate can assist the victim in filling out the paperwork to ensure that they receive the maximum amount of money possible.

A trained professional can also help with making statements to the police and with processing the trauma in a therapeutic setting. If the advocate is not trained to do this, they can refer the victim to a therapist that fits their needs and budget. If the victim is required to appear in court to testify, the advocate can be there to support them and provide a sounding board if necessary.

An arson victim is dealing with an incredible amount of emotional pain. Typically, arson is not a random crime. The offender usually knows their target and wants to hurt the victim and/or destroy their property. A victim advocate can be an invaluable supporter for an arson victim.

Burglary and robbery are two of the most common types of crime. A burglary is when someone breaks into a building with the intention of stealing, hurting someone, or committing unlawful damage.

BURGLARY AND ROBBERY

These two common crimes can be extremely unnerving for victims. Whether the crime was random or the perpetrator specifically targeted the victim's family doesn't necessarily matter—knowing that someone broke into their home, their safe haven, can be a difficult fact to accept. Often, the victims of these crimes feel perpetually on edge, unable to relax even when they are at home, for fear that someone will once again invade their space.

A trained advocate can support those affected by burglary and robbery by aiding them in processing their feelings and taking steps to once again make their home feel like a safe space. This may include directing them to therapy resources, helping them set up a new security system, or supporting them in the prosecution of the perpetrator so that they end up behind bars, unable to rob anyone else.

An advocate can also assist the targeted person in taking inventory of their home and figuring out exactly what is missing, allowing them to thoroughly fill out their police report. The advocate can also help them think through whether they might know the person responsible, aiding police in the successful return of their stolen property.

HATE CRIME

This type of crime is unfathomable to most people, and overcoming the trauma associated with being the victim of a hate crime can be especially difficult. A hate crime is defined as a crime motivated by racial, sexual, or gender prejudice. People who have been victims of hate crimes often struggle with trauma that includes anger, fear, and a general distrust of others.

Victim advocates can be hugely beneficial in

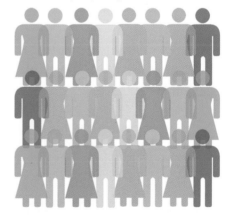

DIFFERENT BUT EQUAL

The term "hate crime" can be used to describe a range of criminal behaviors where the perpetrator is motivated by hostility or demonstrates hostility toward a victim's disability, race, religion, sexual orientation, or transgender identity.

assisting people targeted by hate crimes in facing their offenders and learning how to live life happily once again. Some people who have been victims of hate crimes turn around and become victim advocates for others who are going through the same thing. While all victim advocates receive specialized training, there is something particularly soothing about being assisted by a professional who has been in the same position at some point in their lives, especially when it comes to dealing with hate crimes.

HUMAN TRAFFICKING

Human trafficking is defined as moving men, women, and/or children from one area to another, typically with the intent of exploiting them for sexual or labor purposes.

Human trafficking victim advocates often have to fill a variety of roles. This type of advocacy is unique, as it frequently involves working with victims while crimes are unfortunately still being committed against them. Many human trafficking advisors work on trafficking tip hotlines. Anonymous community members can call in to a hotline and alert the staff of potential human trafficking situations.

Victim advocates might also visit worksites that have been reported to be illegally employing underage workers or establishments that have been reported for conducting illegal sex work. While many people think of human trafficking victims as young

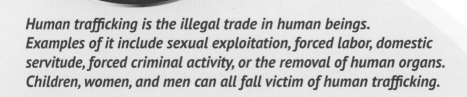

Human trafficking is the illegal trade in human beings. Examples of it include sexual exploitation, forced labor, domestic servitude, forced criminal activity, or the removal of human organs. Children, women, and men can all fall victim of human trafficking.

girls, it's important to remember that anyone—regardless of age, economic status, or gender—can be a victim of these terrible crimes.

A career as an advocate in human trafficking can be a dangerous but important role. Victim advocates in this field often work closely with law enforcement officials to ensure their safety and the safety of the victims they are attempting to protect. When visiting potential human trafficking sites, it is typically essential for advocates to be accompanied by law enforcement officials.

Often, trafficking victims feel trapped by their abuser. Sometimes, they are told that they owe the perpetrator money and that they must work to repay their debt. Many times, those ensnared in trafficking are threatened with violence or injury to their family. Advocates must be understanding of the complex situations that these victims face.

MISSING PERSONS

Victim advocates for missing persons take on a few different roles. They support the family of a missing person throughout the search process, and they might also support the person who was kidnapped or taken against their will after they have been found. If the missing person is not found, they can offer the family resources to manage their grief and find resolution in this seemingly impossible process.

Much like hate crimes, some missing persons advocates have been kidnapped at some point in their lives and have chosen to use their experience to help others. Elizabeth Smart

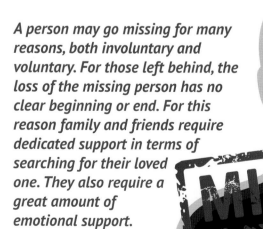

A person may go missing for many reasons, both involuntary and voluntary. For those left behind, the loss of the missing person has no clear beginning or end. For this reason family and friends require dedicated support in terms of searching for their loved one. They also require a great amount of emotional support.

is a well-known example. She was kidnapped and remained missing for nearly a year (2002–2003). Now she uses her story to advocate for victims of abduction and kidnapping.

The AMBER alert program (America's Missing: Broadcast Emergency Response) is an example of the power of victim advocacy in the area of missing persons. Developed in 1996, AMBER alerts immediately let communities know when a child is missing in their area. Countless children have been saved from abduction due to the hard work of victim advocates who created the AMBER alert system.

ASSAULT

It can be difficult for a victim of assault to come forward for a number of reasons, but one of the most common worries expressed by those experiencing an assault is fear of retaliation from their attacker, especially if the offender is someone they know. A victim advocate can encourage the wounded party to find the strength and courage to come forward, as well as provide moral support for the victim if they need to face their attacker in a courtroom setting.

If necessary, an advocate can help the sufferer access protection from law enforcement during the offender's trial.

SEXUAL ABUSE

Sadly, most sexual abuse victims know their abuser. This can make coming forward and reporting sexual abuse exceptionally difficult for victims. Sexual abuse victim advocacy requires patience, understanding, and the ability to support the victim in the decision whether or not to press charges against the

An assault is a violent crime when someone physically hurts or threatens to hurt someone else. Assault also includes crimes where weapons are used. A victim of assault may require protection as well as emotional and medical support.

perpetrator. These professionals can also aid victims in receiving needed medical attention after being abused, and in some cases, the advocate might accompany the victim to their medical appointments. In some states, they can also provide information on emergency contraception if necessary.

Sexual abuse victim advocates must inform those affected of the options they have when it comes to reporting abuse. Professional advocates are also likely to refer victims to therapists who can help them through their trauma, which typically continues long after the crime reporting and subsequent trial have occurred.

Nobody has the right to force another to have sex without their consent. If this happens, it's important to seek help and report the offense to the police.

Sexual abuse trauma is difficult for victims to process. Sometimes, simply having someone there to understand can be helpful. Talking through the trauma and associated feelings is a key part of a sexual abuse victim advocate's job. Many advocates in this field stress that they are able to keep client details confidential, but it's important to note that in some states, information that indicates abuse of children must be shared with law enforcement officials. It's essential that sexual abuse victim advocates have the proper training needed to keep victims safe when a situation must be reported to authorities.

ELDER ABUSE

Elder abuse is not often discussed, but it is unfortunately quite common in the United States. Neglect and abuse run rampant in nursing homes, especially among elderly patients who are bedridden and suffer from ailments that make them unable to speak for themselves. Many elderly individuals are also victims of exploitation, which is the abuse of their money or other financial resources.

Most elder abuse victim advocates work with people who are sixty years of age or older. Sadly, the most common perpetrators of elder abuse are members of the victim's family. In guiding the person through their abusive experience, advocates have to assist the victim in processing any betrayal of trust and deciding what next steps to take.

IDENTITY THEFT

Identity theft is becoming increasingly common in the United States. Identity theft is a crime in which vital pieces of information—such as Social Security numbers and driver's license numbers—are stolen and used to impersonate that person. Often, this information is used to take out loans and credit cards and to obtain services, all while billing the items to the person whose identity has been stolen.

Many people do not know that they've been the victim of identity theft until their monthly credit card bill arrives in the mail. Often, those

Fraudsters are always looking for new ways to hack into computers to steal personal information and data. In the worst situations fraudsters can even steal your identity. Victims of identity theft need special counseling to help them recover emotionally, and they also require practical training to avoid the same thing happening again.

ensnared in identity theft can benefit simply from having someone to talk to. While this crime can affect anyone, victims tend to be older people who are not as technologically advanced as a younger generation.

A victim advocate assists identity theft victims in understanding that what happened to them is not their fault and helps them take steps to lessen the likelihood that this will happen a second time. One of the most frustrating things about identity theft is that perpetrators are rarely caught. This can be difficult for victims to understand.

A trained advocate can help victims recover their losses through their bank or credit card company and process the anger and frustration that come with this type of crime.

HOMICIDE AND ATTEMPTED HOMICIDE

When someone is murdered, the grief that the family feels is incomprehensible. It takes a sensitive, calm, well-educated, and trained professional to even begin to help the family of the deceased process their feelings. While attempted homicide has a less final outcome than homicide, the effects can still be long-lasting and devastating to the victim and their family.

Homicide victim advocates have a variety of objectives. In a homicide attempt, they can support the victims and their families while they talk through their feelings and fears. If the victim is no longer living, they will offer the same support for those left behind. They can help the people affected to protect themselves from further harm by the perpetrator.

Often, victims of attempted homicide are afraid to speak up and press charges due to the fear of retaliation from their attacker. A trained victim advocate can connect the victim with law enforcement and guide them to therapists who can help them to feel safe once again.

When a death has occurred and a murder or manslaughter investigation is underway, it is usually the case that friends and family will be allocated a dedicated caseworker to support all those who have been bereaved.

ADVOCACY IN COURT

For people who have never been inside a courtroom, sitting in front of a judge can feel a little bit intimidating! While going to court can be a part of a victim advocate's job, most of the time, the advocate simply sits in the audience as a supportive, familiar face for the affected person during their testimony.

It's rare that a victim advocate is asked to testify in a case. That being said, it does happen from time to time, so it's important for advocates to be proficient, confident public speakers.

ADVOCATE SPOTLIGHT

See how one victim of violent crime turned her story into something positive by becoming a victim advocate

TEXT-DEPENDENT QUESTIONS

1. What does the acronym AMBER stand for?

2. What are some tasks that an advocate for victims of elder abuse might be asked to complete?

3. List three settings in which a victim advocate might work.

RESEARCH PROJECT

Choose one of the areas described in this chapter, and research what a day in the life of a victim advocate in this field might look like. Be sure to include potential challenges and roadblocks that the advocate might encounter in the field you selected.

Milestone Moment

HUMAN TRAFFICKING

In 2011, President Barack Obama declared January to be Human Trafficking Awareness Month, shining light on a cause that victim advocates fight for every day. Human trafficking refers to the illegal transfer of people that often puts victims into situations involving sexual crime, child labor, and drug activity. President Obama also declared that January 11 would be known as Human Trafficking Awareness Day. Every year, throughout the month of January, trafficking advocates work to raise the public's awareness of human trafficking and the complex issues that its victims face.

HUMAN TRAFFICKING AWARENESS MONTH

Human Trafficking Awareness Month is every January when the issues and problems that victims of human trafficking face are highlighted.

Jim Crow: state and local laws in the southern United States that enforced segregation between black and white people; these laws went into effect in the 1870s and remained in place until the civil rights movement of the 1950s

Ku Klux Klan: a society comprising white American-born Christian men that advocates for white supremacy and is often responsible for hate crimes

segregation: the action of setting a person or group apart from others; often used to describe the separation of black people from white people

socioeconomic status: a social label that is often measured as a combination of education, financial standing, and occupation; it is typically used to measure a person or family's social standing in relation to others in their community

CHAPTER 3

Volunteering and Organizations

VICTIM ADVOCACY ORGANIZATIONS FOR VOLUNTEERING

Across the United States and Canada, there are multiple groups dedicated to victims of different types of crime. Many of these organizations are underfunded and understaffed, and they welcome help from anyone who is willing to volunteer their time or to help raise funds for their cause. When you decide to volunteer, it's critical to choose an

There are a number of jobs you can volunteer for to help victims of crime. Administrative tasks are just as worthwhile and important as hands-on counseling jobs.

issue that you feel passionate about! Volunteer work can be taxing, and it's key that you choose a cause that you'll remain excited about, even when you aren't getting paid.

Volunteering is a wonderful moral endeavor, but it's also a great way to help your college and job applications stand out from the rest. During your volunteer experience, it's a good idea to keep a journal of the tasks you complete and the skills that you gain. Then you will be able to look back later and accurately describe what you learned or did when speaking or writing to a college admissions officer or a potential employer. Most colleges and employers will prefer to see that you spent a significant amount of time volunteering with one organization, rather than a little bit of time at many groups. This is just one more reason why it's so important to choose a charitable foundation that is a good fit for you.

If you know you're interested in victim advocacy but you aren't sure which specialty makes the most sense for you, it's a great idea to spend a few days shadowing volunteers in different areas before you decide to try working in one specialty. Many groups will allow you to spend the day with a volunteer so you can get a sense of the field and see if it's a good match for your needs. Often this shadowing can go hand-in-hand with community service graduation requirements and senior projects. You should ask your school advisor if any paperwork needs to be completed by you, the volunteer organization, or your volunteer supervisor in order for your shadowing to count toward your requirements. Before you begin shadowing, it's also a good idea to write down any questions that you have for the volunteers you will be working with. Some examples to ask might be:

- What's a typical day like for you when you're volunteering?
- What hours do you volunteer throughout the week? Is your schedule flexible?
- What challenges do you face volunteering here? Have you struggled with burnout at all?
- What's the best part of volunteering with this organization?
- What's the most rewarding situation you've been able to participate in as a volunteer?
- Are there opportunities for more responsibility?
- How does this group compare to others that you've volunteered with?

VOLUNTEERS NEEDED

During your time on site with the volunteer, don't forget to ask for business cards from the people you interact with so you know how to contact them later.

After shadowing, writing and sending thank-you notes, both to the

Volunteers are always needed to help support victims of crime. There are numerous vital roles available including providing emotional and practical support, supporting office teams, administration, or raising much-needed funds.

WHAT IF I DON'T WANT TO VOLUNTEER ANYMORE?

It's extremely common for volunteers to feel guilty as they come to the end of their time volunteering with an organization. Sometimes volunteers need to spend more time focusing on their studies, or they are taking on a full-time job to which they need to devote their time. Often this causes volunteers to simply stop showing up for shifts or stop responding to calls and e-mails from the organization. While this method avoids the confrontation of a difficult conversation, it often leaves the organization short-staffed, and ultimately, the victims that the organization is trying to help are the ones who suffer. It's critical to be up front with your supervisor when you decide that your time as a volunteer needs to come to an end. Remember, your supervisor understands that it's unlikely that you'll volunteer forever! Whether it is school, work, or family responsibilities that are getting in the way, just be direct. If you'd like to continue volunteering but need to cut down on your hours, that's Ok! An open, honest conversation with your volunteer leader will be met with appreciation and respect.

organization as a whole and to the volunteers that you shadowed—even if you decide that you're not interested in volunteering with that organization—is a courteous and professional action. Thank them for taking time out of their schedule to show you the ropes, and comment specifically on something that you learned during your time with them.

While any thank-you note is appreciated, resist the temptation to send out something generic. A handwritten note is always more personal than an e-mail, so take the time to actually write a paper note and send it via snail mail.

SEXUAL ASSAULT ORGANIZATIONS

There are many groups that are fighting to raise awareness and create supportive programs for sexual assault and harassment victims. In order to become a volunteer for a sexual assault victim advocacy organization, it's likely that you'll need to undergo a screening process. Depending on their system, you might need to pay for your screening. If this is not possible for you, ask the main office for help—it's likely that they have a fund for helping volunteers get started.

These associations must ensure that their volunteers will uphold their standards of professionalism and confidentiality. The following organizations work with sexual assault victims and for sexual assault prevention.

RAINN

RAINN (Rape, Abuse, & Incest National Network) is the largest anti-sexual violence organization in the United States. Actor Mariska Hargitay has been instrumental in achieving nationwide recognition of RAINN. The

Regardless of nationality and race, both women and men must stand up against sexual violence. Today, there are many organizations that provide advocacy for sexual assault and harassment.

Learn more about how RAINN helps sexual abuse survivors

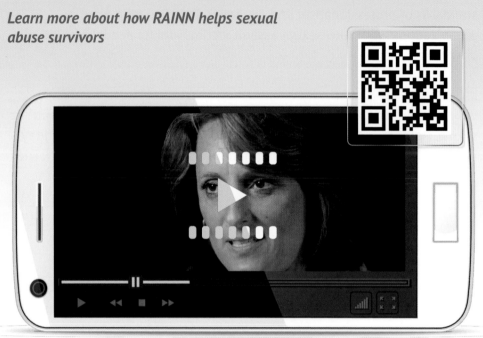

advocates at RAINN are dedicated to getting sexual abuse and assault victims the resources and justice that they deserve. The organization operates a national sexual abuse hotline that connects victims with local therapists and resources so that they are able to stay safe and access proper assistance.

There are very few organizations that operate with the idea of connecting victims to local help. RAINN provides a central telephone number for over-the-phone support and then links victims to local aid agencies so they can get the face-to-face care and medical attention that many of them desperately need. Advocates at RAINN also create programs that prevent sexual violence and bring perpetrators to justice.

Since its creation in 1994, RAINN has helped more than 2.5 million people. The organization is constantly looking for volunteers to go through their training program. After preparation, volunteers are able to staff the hotline and connect victims to local agencies for help. Volunteers can also serve in other capacities with additional instruction.

Not only does RAINN connect victims to their local sexual assault organizations but they also link their volunteers with the community groups. Then they can work on a one-on-one basis with victims, helping them through their trauma and assisting them in a practical way by accompanying them to their medical appointments if necessary.

The #MeToo movement is an international campaign against sexual harassment and assault especially in the workplace. The movement spread virally from its emergence in October 2017 as a hashtag on social media.

CULTURE OF RESPECT

CoR is an organization that promotes sexual assault awareness and prevention on college campuses across the United States. CoR was founded by college students who were fed up with the number of sexual assaults happening on college campuses. Women enrolled in college are three times more likely to be a victim of sexual assault than other women. If there is a college campus in your area, there's a good chance that they already have a Culture of Respect group in place, and if they don't, it's a great idea to start one.

There are a number of volunteer opportunities at CoR, as the organization provides resources not only for sexual assault victims but for friends of victims and children of victims as well. Sometimes, volunteers simply direct those who have experienced a sexual assault (and those who want to help them) to the National Sexual Assault Telephone Hotline. Other times, volunteers might counsel victims on how to press charges after a sexual assault incident or might accompany them to a medical facility following an assault. Volunteers sometimes also assist by answering e-mails from victims who are seeking help in deciding what next steps to take following an assault. CoR volunteers and counselors are also able to direct victims to additional resources they may need, such as professional counseling.

If you are in college, your CoR chapter might be able to help you use your volunteer hours as independent study class credit.

OUR BODIES, OURSELVES

OBOS is an organization that advocates for female reproductive health rights. While OBOS is based in Boston, Massachusetts, they provide information and services to women and girls across the United States. One of the key components of OBOS's mission is to provide information on how a variety of factors—such as age, **socioeconomic** status, and political views—can affect the reproductive care that women and girls receive. OBOS offers both volunteer and internship opportunities for students who want to

Culture of Respect (CoR) is an organization that promotes sexual assault awareness and prevention on college campuses. Volunteers can make an important contribution to CoR simply by helping with calls, redirecting them, or actually providing a victim with support and useful information.

OBOS (Our Bodies, Ourselves) is a nonprofit organization based in Boston, Massachusetts. Its aim is to use education to promote reproductive and sexual health in women and girls.

become involved. Internship opportunities are unpaid, but the time spent and the intern's experiences can be used toward college credit.

Interns and volunteers at OBOS work toward promoting awareness of women's health issues by writing blogs, participating in issue-related conference calls, and attending women's health events. If you're interested in women's rights, women's advocacy, or are thinking about majoring in women's studies in college, an internship or volunteer position at OBOS might be a good fit for you.

HATE CRIME ORGANIZATIONS

SOUTHERN POVERTY LAW CENTER

The SPLC is a well-known, long-standing advocacy organization that has been working to fight hate crimes for years. Founded by civil rights lawyers Morris Dees and Joseph Levin Jr. in 1971, the SPLC has been responsible for a number of landmark legal victories against hate, including ending the last of **Jim Crow segregation**. While the SPLC does have the word "Southern" in its name, it fights against hate crimes across the United States.

The SPLC has two main projects they're working on at this time. The Intelligence Project is an internationally known program that tracks and exposes extremists and hate groups such as the **Ku Klux Klan** (KKK). The SPLC's Hate Map (web address available in the Internet Resources section at the end of this book) shows where specific hate groups, including the KKK, can be found across the country. The map allows people to see that hate crimes and hate groups are in no way a thing of the past—they are very much a modern problem.

A supplementary arrangement, SPLC's Teaching Tolerance program, distributes free materials to schools to reduce bias and increase understanding. The materials can be used in conjunction with the Hate Map.

The SPLC is based in Montgomery, Alabama, and also has satellite offices in Atlanta, Georgia; New Orleans, Louisiana; Miami, Florida; and Jackson, Mississippi. The needs of the SPLC are constantly changing as they continue to address political and social climates, and therefore their volunteer needs are constantly changing as well. The SPLC does not administer high school or undergraduate internships, but they do offer internships to second-year law school students.

The Ku Klux Klan is a group that advocates extremist positions such as white supremacy, white nationalism, and anti-immigration. Although black Americans have typically been the target of this hate group, the Klan has also attacked immigrants, gays, lesbians, Jews, and Catholics.

WE ARE ALL PEOPLE

Hate incidents and hate crimes are acts of violence or hostility directed at people because of who they are or who someone thinks they are. There are many organizations such as ProPublica that work to document hate crimes in an effort to raise awareness of this problem.

PROPUBLICA

ProPublica is an organization that documents hate crimes in an effort to raise awareness and provides advocacy for victims.

Established in 2016, ProPublica creates a place for victims and journalists to connect. By giving victims a platform to share their stories, ProPublica helps those unaware or unaffected by hate crimes to see that these issues are real and that they affect real people every day.

As for volunteer opportunities, ProPublica is always looking for people to help victims of hate crimes write their stories. Sadly, they receive more hate crime tips than they are able to keep up with. Volunteer help is essential to ensure that all the victims' stories will be heard.

ProPublica offers internships to college students.

Human trafficking is the trade of people for exploitation and commercial gain. The Polaris Project is a project whose aim is to free women and girls from human trafficking networks. There are many different volunteering roles available with Polaris.

HUMAN TRAFFICKING ORGANIZATIONS

POLARIS PROJECT

The Polaris Project gets its name from the North Star. Before the Civil War, slaves used the North Star to guide their escape from the southern United States and out of slavery. The Polaris Project's mission is similar—to free women and girls from the human trafficking networks that rob them of their freedom.

Victim advocates at Polaris work in three different ways: They use technology to locate and prosecute offenders, they work one-on-one with trafficking survivors, and they promote awareness of human trafficking to eradicate this modern-day slavery. While many people think of human trafficking as only involving young girls, it can also involve underpaid foreign workers and child labor.

It might be hard to believe that these terrible conditions exist in the United States and Canada; therefore, Polaris is currently running a variety of initiatives to raise awareness of the problem. They are also attempting to stop human trafficking from taking place in hotels, factories, massage parlors, and more.

Typically, 200–300 applications are received, and only 10–20 students are selected for the program.

To learn more about how to increase your chances of winning an internship with The Polaris Project, get in touch with their office. Their contact information is in the back of this book.

A21 is a nonprofit organization that campaigns to free people from modern-day slavery. This protest rally took place in London, England.

Volunteering with Polaris can take a number of different forms, and responsibilities range from filling out paperwork to accompanying victims to medical appointments. The Polaris Project offers internships to students who show leadership qualities and who are dedicated to ending human trafficking. This internship program is heralded as an incredible, in-depth learning experience for students, and so the application process is very competitive.

Modern slavery is often associated with women and girls who are forced to work in the sex industry. However, men and boys are also at risk.

URBAN LIGHT

Urban Light has an interesting story. Alezandra Russell founded the organization in 2009 after a trip to Thailand, where she witnessed the open sex trafficking of young boys firsthand. She decided to do something about it, and immediately upon her return to her home in Washington, DC, she began raising funds to start Urban Light.

Boys and young men are often left out of the conversation when it comes to human trafficking, but they are subject to these horrors alongside girls and women. Urban Light is a victim advocacy group that works to bring awareness to the problem of trafficking men and boys. This organization is located in Thailand, where sex trafficking crimes are at an all-time high. Urban Light also works with young trafficking victims who are homeless and have substance abuse issues.

Urban Light is an organization founded in 2009 to help young boys who are trafficked for sex. It helps to empower the boys to pursue a life outside the horrors of exploitation and trafficking.

GETTING INVOLVED

If you're interested in volunteering as a victim advocate for a specific cause, it's a great idea to start out by contacting your local courthouse and/or police department to ask how you can help. The advocacy unit there will be able to direct you to organizations in your area that advocate in the cause you're interested in. If your church has a youth group, your youth group leader will likely also be able to point you in the right direction. And school guidance counselors can guide you to the first steps for getting involved.

When you're talking to the organization, don't be afraid to tell them that you're a student. Many professional organizations welcome student volunteers and interns!

VOLUNTEERING IN PERSON

While virtual volunteering is wonderful, there is nothing that can replace the firsthand experience of volunteering in person. Being face-to-face with

When volunteering in person you will be able to meet with victims. It may be that you will be asked to undertake simple tasks such as making the victim a drink or offering support until a qualified person becomes free.

For those wanting to help victims of crime, it is important to carefully research the role you want to perform. A group discussion with a professionally trained victim advocate will help guide you through the process of choosing your preferred role.

victims is not only helpful for the victim but it's also a great way to figure out if the field of victim advocacy is a good fit for you. There are a variety of opportunities at the nonprofit organizations listed above for in-person volunteering.

Remember that as a volunteer, you're there to support the organization, not necessarily dive right into the work you're most interested in. When you meet with your supervisor before you begin your volunteer commitment, it's important to get an idea of the kind of work you'll be expected to do to ensure that the opportunity is a good fit for your needs.

If you live near an organization that you'd like to volunteer with, you can typically select your own days and hours to volunteer. Some organizations require travel and a longer commitment, such as the Urban Light organization mentioned previously. They require travel to Thailand and a six-month commitment.

If you are interested in a travel volunteer experience, it's a good idea to talk to your school counselor to see if you can arrange to have class credit given for your volunteer time. Many high schools and colleges love this type of real-world experience and will work with you to make it happen.

While volunteer work is by definition unpaid, remember that the organization is relying on you to fulfill a need when you volunteer. Volunteers need to treat their assignments the same way they would treat a paid job. This means showing up on time

Offering kind words and providing reassurance to the victim is very important after a crime.

for your shift, working hard, asking questions when you need help, and letting your supervisor know well in advance if you are unable to work during a scheduled time. As a volunteer, you're there to learn and to help. While you might think you have the answers for how to handle situations with victims, always run your ideas by your supervisor or an experienced volunteer.

A victim of crime requires emotional support and practical information. Contacting a reputable helpline is a good way of getting sound advice and support.

A helpline is a telephone service that offers help to those in need. In addition to telephone support, helplines provide useful information and organizations to contact. These can be followed-up independently once the victim hangs up.

HOTLINE SERVICE

Volunteers man many victim advocacy hotlines. People who call these hotlines are in a variety of situations. Some of them might be calling to get

If you decide to volunteer at a helpline center, before you start work you will receive special training to prepare you for all the kinds of calls you are likely to receive.

help in figuring out if they are being abused. Others might call the hotline after they have already reported a crime to the police and find themselves in need of additional support. They also might be calling to report potential abuse against children or the elderly. When volunteering on a hotline, it's vital to pay close attention during your training and remember that your job is to support the caller.

Often, you'll encounter situations where you believe the caller needs support beyond what the hotline can provide. Your supervisor or volunteer leader will give you instructions on how to report these cases to ensure that the caller is safe and receives the necessary services. These types of calls can be difficult to handle emotionally. Later, you might wonder what happened to the caller or if your support was enough. Remember that just by volunteering, you are providing exactly what the caller needs in their time of crisis—a listening ear and assistance.

Many organizations now also offer text message support. If you're a budding counselor or psychiatrist, this might be something that you are interested in. Most text support hotlines require that volunteers go through training at their own pace and that they sign up for two-hour shifts (at their convenience). If you're interested in volunteering but struggle with transportation

Active listeners are good listeners. A victim advocate must have excellent listening ability, patience, and understanding. They must be able to allow a victim to express their concerns and worries about the hurt they are feeling as a victim of crime.

WHAT IF I WANT MORE RESPONSIBILITY?

After you've spent some time learning the ropes, you might begin to feel like you're ready for additional volunteer responsibility. The best thing you can do is go to your supervisor or volunteer leader and let them know that you'd like to explore handling more responsibility. If the people in charge decide that they have some areas of growth for you to work on before you are given more responsibility, or if you need additional training, do not take offense! Instead, be appreciative for the opportunity to learn more. Work hard and track your progress, and come back to your supervisor in a few months with proof of growth.

or don't have a lot of time, text message crisis services might be a good place for you to start. Just like with in-person volunteering, you should keep a log of your hours if you plan to use them for a community service or graduation requirement. Talk with your counselor or college advisor to make sure text crisis counseling is an acceptable form of volunteer service.

Volunteering can be taxing, and it's important that you make your own self-care a priority while working as a victim advocate volunteer. Pay close attention to your own stress levels, and don't be afraid to talk to a counselor if you find yourself struggling to handle the situations you encounter with your callers. Remember, you can't help others without first helping yourself. It's normal to feel overwhelmed as a volunteer, and your supervisor or volunteer leader will be able to help you through it.

TEXT-DEPENDENT QUESTIONS

1. What are two reasons that someone would call a crisis hotline?

2. What is one question that you should ask someone when you are shadowing them?

3. Where are the Southern Poverty Law Center offices located?

RESEARCH PROJECT

Choose one of the organizations listed in this chapter, and research its backstory. When was it founded, and by whom? Why did they decide to start the organization? How has the initiative grown over time? Write a two-page report on the organization's history, and share it with your class.

Milestone Moment

NATIONAL CRIME VICTIMS' SERVICE AWARD

On April 13, 2018, the National Crime Victims' Service Award ceremony was held in Washington, DC, to celebrate the accomplishments of victim advocates across the nation. In the past, victim advocacy was looked at mainly as a volunteer position, but the field is quickly gaining more recognition. Each year, eleven different awards are given to people who stand out in the field, including the Volunteer for Victims Award and the Tomorrow's Leaders Award. The National Crime Victims' Service Award is important in letting victim advocates understand that their daily work is extremely important and valued by many.

The National Crime Victims' Service Awards are presented to individuals, organizations, teams, or programs that demonstrate outstanding achievement in supporting victims of crime.

graduate degree: a level of education that is obtained after a student completes their first four years of college (thus earning a bachelor's degree); includes master's and doctorate degrees

social issues: any problem that affects a large number of people in a society, such as crime, homelessness, or education

social work: the field of study that focuses on disadvantaged individuals in a society and how their welfare can be improved

CHAPTER 4

Education, Training, and Qualifications

HOW TO BECOME A VICTIM ADVOCATE

There are many different avenues that you can take toward becoming a victim advocate. First you need to decide if you'd like to pursue advocacy as a volunteer or as a lifelong career. While both goals are valuable, only one will allow you to make money.

One of the first things that you need to do when choosing a career as a victim advocate is deciding which field you'd like to enter. Some advocates work for courthouses and support victims who are experiencing many different types of crimes. Others work for organizations that specialize in one area, such as human trafficking or hate crimes. All advocacy work is valuable, but you'll do your best work when you are helping a population that means a lot to you.

In some difficult cases, when a victim of crime has been very badly affected, a professionally qualified social worker will provide the necessary support.

If you're not sure whether you'd like to specialize in one area or not, that's ok. Your training, studies, and volunteer involvement will open your eyes to a variety of **social issues** and victim experiences. It's likely that you'll eventually find yourself drawn to a certain advocacy area.

VOLUNTEER VS. CAREER

If you choose to pursue victim advocacy as a volunteer, the training and education requirements will vary depending on what organization you choose to work with. Some organizations will insist that you have a certain education level, while others might simply require that you go through trainings that they have created. Just like with any position, as you gain more responsibility, it's likely that your level of training will need to increase. Some organizations pay for volunteer training, while others require you to pay a fee or apply for a scholarship.

As a volunteer, the amount of time you want to invest and your level of involvement with the organization is up to you. If you're not sure whether victim advocacy is the right career path for you, volunteering is a great way to find out. Many organizations first offer jobs to promising volunteers before allowing the job posting to be seen by the general public.

If you choose to pursue victim advocacy as a career, the training and education required will be much more intense than if you were working as a volunteer. There are a few different college majors that you could enroll in that could lead to a career in victim advocacy, including criminal justice, psychology, **social work**, women's studies, education, or child development. When choosing your major, talk with your high school or college advisor about which route makes the most sense for you to become a victim advocate. Various schools have different course requirements for similar majors, and it's likely that your advisor will be able to recommend a path that will lead you to a career in advocacy.

Victim advocates are almost always identified as "mandated reporters," meaning they need to report to their supervisor or to the authorities if someone is in danger. Child abuse and neglect are also situations that are mandated to be reported. Your supervisor will go over how to determine when something needs to be reported. If you are ever unsure of whether or not you should report something—either as a volunteer or as a paid victim advocate—you should check with your supervisor.

If you decide to pursue victim advocacy as a career, the required training will be intensive and hard work. However, once qualified, you will find your chosen career both rewarding and interesting.

HELP! THE ORGANIZATION I WANT TO WORK WITH ISN'T ACCEPTING NEW VOLUNTEERS AT THIS TIME

While this can be frustrating, you might also view it as an opportunity to gain experience in another specialty area. If the organization you'd like to work with isn't currently accepting new volunteers, ask them to recommend other organizations in your area that do similar work, and ask them to place you on their waiting list for when new volunteer opportunities arise. It's also a good idea to call back regularly—once a month or so—to see if their volunteer needs have changed. Even if they still aren't accepting new people, your persistence will stand out to the volunteer coordinator and increase the odds that you'll be first to get a call when a need opens up.

VICTIM ADVOCATES AND THE CRIMINAL JUSTICE SYSTEM

In Canada, many government organizations are beginning to realize the important role that victim advocates play in the criminal justice system

EDUCATION AND TRAINING

For volunteer positions, most organizations will assign duties based on your education level. A volunteer with more education and experience is likely to be given more responsibility than a volunteer who is just starting out in the field. For paid positions, there is a similar pattern. An employee who has just completed their bachelor's degree will not have as much responsibility as an employee who has years of experience and a **graduate degree**.

Keep in mind that everyone has to start somewhere, and it's ok if you aren't given much responsibility at the beginning of your career. Your level of responsibility and your experience will grow with time! If you're interested in working to earn more responsibility, either as a volunteer or a paid advocate, let your supervisor know. They might want to send you to

Support groups offer mentoring and weekly workshops for victims of crime. These meetings help to promote improved mental health and recovery.

trainings on leadership so that as your experience grows, you'll be able to transition into a leadership position easily.

As mentioned above, there are many different college majors that can lead to a career in victim advocacy. Each major will have its own course of study, although many will have class and internship requirements overlaps, and will lend itself to different types of advocacy. Some fields, such as criminal justice, provide enough training that it makes sense to dive into courtroom advocacy right away. Other fields, such as social work, might require a graduate degree to really delve into advocacy work.

If you're interested in a specialty—such as working only with women or children—it might make sense for you to have a streamlined major and minor. Your college advisor will be able to help you decide which path makes the most sense for you and your goals. Some organizations will pay for employees to pursue graduate-level education.

Typically, getting this type of scholarship requires the employee to sign a contract agreeing to continue working with the organization for a certain number of years after the graduate education is completed. Often, the contract also stipulates that the payment for the education will continue only if the employee maintains a certain grade point average.

Regardless of which major path you choose, internships and volunteering are a hugely important part of advocacy training. Some people interested in advocacy go

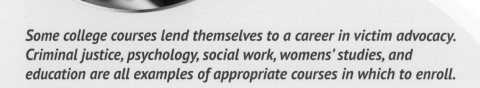

Some college courses lend themselves to a career in victim advocacy. Criminal justice, psychology, social work, womens' studies, and education are all examples of appropriate courses in which to enroll.

Throughout your chosen career in helping victims of crime, you will often have to attend training courses from time to time to keep abreast of up-to-date procedures and methods of working.

through an internship or a volunteer experience and realize that the field actually isn't a good fit—and that's ok! Advocacy is emotional, taxing, and difficult work, and it's important to be sure that it's a field in which you feel fulfilled and comfortable.

In the United States, many advocacy organizations require advocates to become certified by the National Organization for Victims Assistance (NOVA). This association offers different levels of certification based on education and experience level. Often, advocacy groups will pay for their advocates to get certification.

QUALIFICATIONS

As with any public service position, it's likely that you will need to pass a background check in order to become a victim advocate. The rules on this vary depending on the organization that you work with, and some groups are likely to make exceptions depending on an advocate's particular situation. For example, if an advocate got into the field because they were once a trafficking victim and were charged for related crimes, an

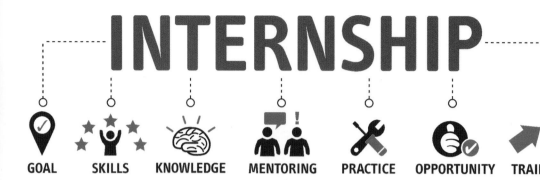

INTERNSHIP

GOAL **SKILLS** **KNOWLEDGE** **MENTORING** **PRACTICE** **OPPORTUNITY** **TRAINING**

The most important advantage of an unpaid internship in victim support is the experience it provides. If you choose to spend your summer in an unpaid internship to gain knowledge about this particular field, you will inevitably benefit from the time you spend doing so.

organization will probably be inclined to overlook those charges. Honesty is always the best policy when it comes to past issues, though, and employers are likely to be more understanding if an issue is brought to their attention before a background check is processed. You will also need to be fingerprinted. Your fingerprints will be kept on file with the state government.

Many advocacy positions also require a number of years of experience. It's key to have volunteer positions on your resume. Many organizations are happy to count volunteering as job experience. This is why it's key to have good relationships with your volunteer supervisors. Often, employers will call volunteer supervisors as a reference to get a sense of the potential

> *A well-qualified professional will always command a good salary and with hard work will be able to build a fulfilling career.*

JOB SEARCH

FIND JOB

are stuck in the throes of the criminal justice system. When interviewing for a victim advocacy position, it is helpful to explain any unique experiences you have to your interviewer. Those situations can take the place of years of experience in certain situations.

Victims come from all sectors of society, and all require equal attention, regardless of their circumstances.

employee's responsibility, dependability, work ethic, etc. When the potential employer sees that you were willing to give your all as a volunteer, they'll know that you'll be willing to go above and beyond the call of duty as an employee.

Victim advocacy is a unique field because many professionals have experience on the other side—they were once victims themselves. While being the victim of a crime can be incredibly scarring, it can also provide unique insights into the needs of people who

As with other public service jobs, it is likely that you will need to pass a background check in order to start a career working with victims of crime.

HOW DOES VICTIM ADVOCACY RESPONSIBILITY CHANGE WITH EXPERIENCE?

Whether you choose to enter the victim advocacy field as a volunteer or a paid professional, your responsibilities will change as you gain more experience. Experienced advocates are often responsible for the training and supervision of advocates who are just getting started in the field. With more knowledge, you'll be able to counsel advocates who are learning the ropes. It takes time to feel comfortable in a supervisory role, and it's likely that the organization you work with will provide leadership training to help you better navigate these new responsibilities.

When working with victims you will spend many hours providing emotional and practical support. It is therefore important that you are comfortable in your clothing as well as being neat and tidy.

TEXT-DEPENDENT QUESTIONS

1. What are two potential college majors for someone who is interested in becoming a victim advocate?

2. What should you do if the organization you want to volunteer with is not currently accepting new volunteers?

3. Is graduate school necessary to become a victim advocate?

RESEARCH PROJECT

Choose one of the college majors listed in this chapter, and research the classes and internships required to complete the major at a college or university of your choice. Create a drawing that starts where you are now and shows the path you can take to achieve your goal.

Milestone Moment

THE #METOO MOVEMENT

On October 15, 2017, the #MeToo movement exploded onto the social media scene. On that day, actor Alyssa Milano posted on Twitter and encouraged others to use the tag and come forward with their previously hidden stories of sexual assault and harassment. The popularity of the movement was considered a victory for advocacy, as it raised awareness and put faces to what is often a secret, hidden crime.

Participants in a demonstration against sexism under the #MeToo Movement in Malmö, Sweden.

cost of living: the cost of basic necessities as defined by an accepted standard—such as food, drink, clothing, household supplies and personal care items, home rents, and transportation often used when comparing how expensive it is to live in one location versus another

safety plan: since many victims fear for their safety after a trauma, a safety plan is a list of steps that they can take when they feel that they are once again in danger, which might include calling their advocate, relocating to stay with a relative, staying in a hotel, etc.

stalking: unwanted contact that occurs between two people and places the victim in a state of fear or unrest

CHAPTER 5

Salaries, Job Outlook, and Work Satisfaction

SALARIES

Victim advocate salaries vary widely and are often based on education and experience. Location also plays a role in salary. In areas with a higher **cost of living**, such as a city environment, victim advocates are typically paid more than in areas with a lower cost of living, such as a rural location. On average, victim advocates make $58,410 per year. Victim advocates in the top 10 percent of the salary range can make more than $85,000 per year. These salary ranges do not include any perks, such as paid education

WILL I BE ABLE TO FIND A JOB AS AN ADVOCATE?

The field of victim advocacy is currently experiencing growth, as many social justice organizations are beginning to recognize the value in having staff members who are trained in the psychology and trauma that victims go through while reporting crimes and while participating in court cases. There are many things that you can do in high school and college to increase your chances of getting hired after you finish your advocacy training. Internships, volunteer opportunities, unrequired courses, and independent study can all make it more likely that you'll get hired by the organization of your choice after you finish your education.

#METOO MOVEMENT

Learn more about the #MeToo movement and how it has changed the way many people look at sexual assault and harassment

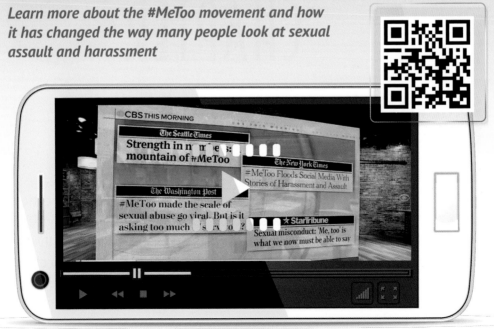

or training. Government organizations, both federal and local, typically pay victim advocates more than private organizations.

JOB OUTLOOK

It's likely that the field of victim advocacy will continue to experience steady growth in the coming years. Unfortunately, crime does not appear to be decreasing in the United States and Canada, and crime statistics support this. The victims of the crimes need advocates to fight for their rights and to help them get compensation and justice.

Government offices continue to recognize victim advocates as a key part of a successful criminal justice system, and each year, more and more government offices are willing to pay social workers and counselors to work solely in this field. Many state and local governments are working to improve their victim compensation programs, and advocates are needed

Job satisfaction is a measure of how content a worker is in his or her career.

to help governments understand the financial needs of victims. Professionals are also necessary to walk victims through these systems to get their needs fulfilled.

In addition to a college degree, many employers look for extra skills in victim advocate, including compassion, patience, the ability to work well under pressure, the ability to stay calm in emotionally difficult situations, the ability to work well with tight deadlines, public speaking skills, and information technology skills. Proficiency or training in these areas can increase the likelihood of getting hired as a victim advocate and can be used to leverage a higher salary offer.

A day in the life of a person working as a victim advocate can include many tasks such as referring a person to a counselor, organizing childcare, and organizing a victim's medical care among other things.

WORK SATISFACTION

Many victim advocates feel a deep sense of satisfaction with the work they do, especially when victims come back years later to explain what a difference the advocate made in their life. While these moments are incredible, the day-to-day stress of working with victims can take its toll.

One of the most difficult parts of the job is being unable to help certain victims. Advocates must recognize that they are not going to be able to solve or fix all situations. Many people enter the field because of a

For every victim you support, each will have case notes that have to be regularly updated and actioned.

personal experience with being a victim of a crime. These memories can make it difficult for advocates to hear about crime and violence on a daily basis. In addition, while some victim advocates work a typical 9 to 5 weekday schedule, many are frequently called into work after hours. This is especially common with advocates who work with domestic violence and

Victim advocates must often work closely with the police.

When a victim has suffered a physical injury, it may be necessary to arrange for them to be taken to a hospital. If they are admitted, it is likely that a victim advocate will visit them for support sessions.

sexual assault victims. Medical appointments with these victims can occur on the weekends and very late at night or early in the morning. This can take a toll on the advocate's personal and family life. In some areas of the country, victim advocates have a very large caseload, making it almost impossible to attend to the needs of all victims falling under the advocate's jurisdiction. This leads to high levels of stress for the advocate.

Victims advocates need to have some understanding of the law and will often have to liaise with a legal professional on behalf of the victims they support.

Helping a victim to talk about a traumatic experience requires a lot of tact and experience. At times such as these, the victim advocate called upon will usually be a senior member of staff.

A successful victim advocate will be trained in how to cope with stressful and difficult situations.

When interviewing for an advocacy position, it's important to fully understand the expectations of the role. Some organizations expect advocates to be on call regularly, while others allow a more typical schedule. Some organizations need advocates to testify in court, while others do not expect them to ever enter a courtroom. Asking questions not only helps you understand if the job is a good fit, but it also shows the interviewer that you've researched the role and understand the position.

SELF-CARE

As mentioned previously, the burnout rate is high in the field of victim advocacy. Many professionals dedicate so much time to their work that they neglect taking care of themselves.

Coping with traumatic and sometimes life-changing situations can take its toll on a victim advocate.

The job is emotionally taxing, as most advocates deal with situations involving violence and abuse on a daily basis.

Some advocates feel that since they counsel others, they do not need supportive therapy for themselves, but this is not true. Advocates need to seek counseling and take plenty of time off to allow themselves to reset. Visiting a therapist does not mean that the advocate is weak or unable to do their job. Processing the feelings associated with victims and crime is one of the best ways to promote mental health and accomplish being a great advocate for others. It's easy to fall into the trap of thinking that working more

For those with busy and demanding work lives, it is essential to look after one's mental health by taking time out to relax.

COPING WITH WORK-RELATED STRESS

When working as a victim advocate, you will come in contact with people who have suffered greatly, often both physically and mentally. It is therefore essential that you manage your own mental health carefully so that you can adequately cope with the job in hand. If you think you are suffering from stress, it is important that you act quickly. Speaking to your employer or someone else you trust is the first thing you should consider doing. He or she will be in a position to understand what you are going through and advise you accordingly. There are a number of ways to avoid work-related stress. These include balancing your time, being realistic about your work-related goals, and remembering to take breaks and time off. You should always reward yourself for good achievements and remember to nurture good relationships with your colleagues.

Working with victims is a rewarding job where you are helping others to overcome difficult, traumatic, and even life-threatening experiences.

DAY IN THE LIFE: VICTIM ADVOCATE

One of the most exciting things about working as a victim advocate is that no two days are the same! Each day provides new challenges, new people to work with, and new positive outcomes. When a crime occurs, the first step for an advocate is to reach out to the victim and assess their needs. Do they need a referral to a counselor? Do they need help with providing food for their children? Your job is to meet these immediate needs and those that arise afterward. If requested, you might accompany the victim to a medical appointment, if that makes sense for the crime they are dealing with. You might be responsible for appearing in court to support a victim. It's likely that you'll also check in with past victims, ensuring that they have a safety plan in place if necessary to protect them from their offender, especially in the case of stalking. Even weeks or months after a crime has occurred, many victims still need the support of their advocate. It's often difficult for victims to move forward with their lives, and advocates might help them do this by helping them seek employment, arrange for transportation and childcare, and engage in hobbies. Like most jobs, you will probably need to file paperwork and attend meetings regularly throughout the week.

hours creates a better situation for victims, but nothing could be further from the truth. Advocates can do their best work only when they are mentally and physically healthy, and rest is an important part of health.

While it can be difficult, it's crucial for advocates to talk to their supervisors and colleagues if they feel their mental health is suffering. A supervisor would prefer that an employee come to them seeking help instead of burning out to the point where they are no longer able to do their job effectively—or at all. Asking for help is a sign of strength, not a sign of weakness.

TEXT-DEPENDENT QUESTIONS

1. How much does a victim advocate get paid per year on average?

2. What qualities does an employer look for in a potential victim advocate?

3. Why must a victim advocate look after their own mental health?

RESEARCH PROJECT

Choose two of the organizations from the back of this book, and reach out to them to ask if you can interview one of their victim advocates. Ask each advocate to walk you through a typical day at work. Compare and contrast the two experiences.

SERIES GLOSSARY OF KEY TERMS

abuse: Wrong or unfair treatment or use.

academic: Of or relating to schools and education.

advancement: Progression to a higher stage of development.

anxiety: Fear or nervousness about what might happen.

apprentice: A person who learns a job or skill by working for a fixed period of time for someone who is very good at that job or skill.

culture: A way of thinking, behaving, or working that exists in a place or organization (such as a business.)

donation: The making of an especially charitable gift.

empathy: The ability to understand and share the feelings of others.

endangered species: A specific type of plant or animal that is likely to become extinct in the near future.

ethics: The study of morality, or right and wrong.

food security: Having reliable access to a steady source of nutritious food.

intern: A student or recent graduate in a special field of study (as medicine or teaching) who works for a period of time to gain practical experience.

mediation: Intervention between conflicting parties to promote reconciliation, settlement, or compromise.

nonprofit: A charitable organization that uses its money to help others, rather than to make financial gain, aka "profit."

ombudsman: A person who advocates for the needs and wants of an individual in a facility anonymously so that the individual receiving care can voice complaints without fear of consequences.

pediatrician: A doctor who specializes in the care of babies and children.

perpetrator: A person who commits a harmful or illegal act.

poverty: The state of one who lacks a usual or socially acceptable amount of money or material possessions.

retaliate: To do something bad to someone who has hurt you or treated you badly; to get revenge against someone.

salary: The amount of money you receive each year for the work you perform.

sanctuary: A place of refuge and protection.

stress: Something that causes strong feelings of worry or anxiety.

substance abuse: Excessive use of a drug (such as alcohol, narcotics, or cocaine); use of a drug without medical justification.

syndrome: A group of signs and symptoms that occur together and characterize a particular abnormality or condition.

therapist: A person trained in methods of treatment and rehabilitation other than the use of drugs or surgery.

ORGANIZATIONS TO CONTACT

Culture of Respect: 1111 K St. NE, 10th Floor, Washington, DC 20002. Phone: (202) 265-7500 E-mail: office@naspa.org Website: www.naspa.org

National Center for Victims of Crime: 2000 M St. NW #480, Washington, DC 20036. Phone: (202) 467-8700 Fax: (202) 467-8701 Website: www.victimsofcrime.org

National Organization for Victim Assistance: 510 King St., Suite 424, Alexandria, VA 22314. Phone: (703) 535-6682 Fax: (703) 535-5500 Website: www.trynova.org

Our Bodies, Ourselves: P.O. Box 590403, Newton Center, MA 02459. Phone: (617) 425-0200 E-mail: office@ourbodiesourselves.org Website: www.ourbodiesourselves.org

ProPublica: 155 Avenue of the Americas, 13th Floor, New York, NY 10013. Phone: (212) 514-5250 Fax: (212) 785-2634 E-mail: hello@propublica.org Website: www.propublica.org

Polaris: P.O. Box 65323, Washington, DC 20035. Phone: (202) 790-6300 E-mail: info@polarisproject.org Website: www.polarisproject.org

RAINN: 1220 L St. NW, Washington, DC 20005. Phone: (202) 544-1034 Website: www.rainn.org

Southern Poverty Law Center: 400 Washington Ave., Montgomery, AL 36104. Phone: (888) 414-7752 Website: www.splcenter.org

Urban Light: For the safety of victims, the address of Urban Light is not public information. Phone: (301) 523-0187 Website: www.urban-light.org

INTERNET RESOURCES

https://crcvc.ca/
The Canadian Resource Center for Victims of Crime provides resources and services to victims of crime in Canada.

https://www.crimevictims.gov/volunteers.html
The CrimeVictims website provides valuable resources on victim advocacy programs and volunteer opportunities.

https://suicidepreventionlifeline.org/participate/
The National Suicide Prevention hotline is a key resource for victim advocates. Many victim advocates get their start in the field by volunteering for a suicide prevention hotline.

http://www.victimsfirst.gc.ca/serv/vsc-svc.html
Victims First provides Canadian crime victims and their families with a variety of resources to aid in their recovery, including financial compensation for certain victims.

https://www.volunteermatch.org
Ready to volunteer, but not sure where to start? The Volunteer Match database allows you to search for organizations in your area that are looking for volunteers. You'll be able to choose if you're looking for a place to physically go and volunteer, or if you prefer work that you can do from your computer or phone.

FURTHER READING

Cunningham, David. *Klansville, U.S.A.: The Rise and Fall of the Civil Rights-Era Ku Klux Klan*. Oxford, UK: Oxford University Press, 2014.

Johnston, Tate. *Everyday Abolitionist: What You Can Do To Stop Modern Slavery/ Human Trafficking*. London: Everyday Abolitionist Press, 2018.

Kolb, Kenneth. *Moral Wages: The Emotional Dilemmas of Victim Advocacy and Counseling*. Oakland, CA: University of California Press, 2014.

Phoenix, Olga. *Victim Advocate's Guide to Wellness: Six Dimensions of Vicarious Trauma-Free Life*. North Charleston, SC: CreateSpace Independent Publishing Platform, 2014.

Smart, Elizabeth. *Where There's Hope: Healing, Moving Forward, and Never Giving Up*. New York: St. Martin's Press, 2018.

Southern Poverty Law Center. *Keeping the Dream Alive: The Cases and Causes of the Southern Poverty Law Center*. Montgomery, AL: Southern Poverty Law Center, 2014.

Tripodi, Lois. *Trafficked: Two Sisters Lost*. Portsmouth, NH: Piscataqua Press, 2014.

Yousafzai, Malala. *I Am Malala: The Girl Who Stood Up for Education and Was Shot by the Taliban*. Boston: Back Bay Books, 2015.

INDEX

AUTHOR'S BIOGRAPHY

AMANDA TURNER is a children's book author and former middle school teacher. Elizabeth is passionate about helping students discover what field they'd like to pursue in college and beyond. In her spare time, she enjoys vacationing in Bermuda with her family. She lives in Dayton, Ohio, with her husband, son, dog, and cat.

CREDITS